Circus

Written by April George

CONTENTS

Rigby®

HOUGHTON MIFFLIN HARCOURT

Circus Science

Circus performers may look like daredevils, but they think like scientists. They understand the science behind their acts. They know what makes their acts work and what will make them fail. *A circus is science at work.*

Flying High

Trapeze artists swing because of forces. Forces are pushes and pulls that make things move. The trapeze will not start swinging until the artist pushes off from the platform. The harder the trapeze artist pushes off, the faster the trapeze will swing. When the trapeze slows down, the artist swings back to the platform and pushes off again.

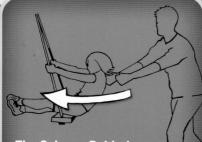

The Science Behind the Act: Force

Still objects stay still until a force moves them. An object will increase its speed more quickly if the force is stronger.

The harder you push off the platform, the faster you will swing.

It takes a lot of practice to do this.

Juggling

Circus jugglers can juggle many objects at once. This is because the objects fall at the same speed. A force called gravity pulls all objects toward Earth. When a juggler throws a ball into the air, gravity pulls it down again. The harder the juggler throws the ball, the higher and faster it will go.

Jugglers often learn to juggle using scarves because they catch more air and fall slowly.

Ball thrown with most force

Ball thrown with least force

The Science Behind the Act: Gravity

Gravity is constant. This means an object does not fall faster today than it did yesterday because objects fall at the same speed.

To juggle many objects at the same time, a juggler must throw some with more force than the others. This makes the objects come down at different times, allowing the juggler to keep all the objects moving.

Some jugglers spin plates on top of thin sticks. Why don't the plates fall off? The reason is centripetal force. This force happens when an object spins so fast that it resists the pull of gravity. It is the same force that lets you ride a bike. While the bike is moving, you stay upright, but if you stop moving, you fall over. As long as the juggler keeps the plates spinning, the plates will stay on top of the sticks.

The Science Behind the Act: Centripetal Force

A spinning object is more stable than a still object. While the top is spinning, it stays upright.

Tightrope Feats

To be a tightrope artist takes years of training. To keep their balance on a tightrope, artists must keep their center of gravity directly above the wire. If they lean to one side, gravity will make them fall in that direction. Often, tightrope artists use a long pole to help them keep balanced.

The Science Behind the Act: Center of Gravity

Every object has a center of gravity. Balance a pair of scissors on a bottle. The center of gravity is not always the middle of the object.

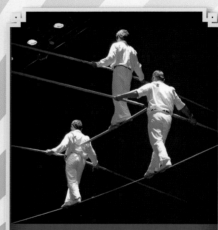

Often several artists will work together. Each performer must be careful to mind the center of gravity in the act. Every time a performer moves, the center of gravity moves, too.

Acrobatic Feats

Acrobats bend, twist, leap, and turn somersaults. They climb and bend to form a tower. Acrobats use energy to perform their feats. This energy is stored in their muscles and fat. When the acrobats are still, they have potential energy, and when they begin to move, the energy changes form. It is called movement or kinetic energy.

Acrobats need to train every day because their bodies must be strong to keep balanced.

The Science Behind the Act: Energy

Energy can change from one form to another. Most energy on Earth comes from the sun.

Plants get energy from the sun to make food.

People get energy when they eat plants and animals that have eaten plants.

Our bodies store this energy in muscle and fat. It is potential energy.

When we move, we release the energy. It becomes movement or kinetic energy.

13

The Lights and Sounds of the Circus

Lighting is used at a circus to make the acts look stunning. Lighting workers mix different colored lights to make beautiful effects.

Light is a kind of energy that travels like a wave. The color of the light depends on its wavelength. When light of two different colors is mixed together, their wavelengths are combined, making new colors.

The Science Behind the Act: Light

The primary colors of light are red, green, and blue. Light of these three colors can be mixed together to make other colors. When all the colors are mixed together, we see white light.

Blue lighting creates a mysterious mood.

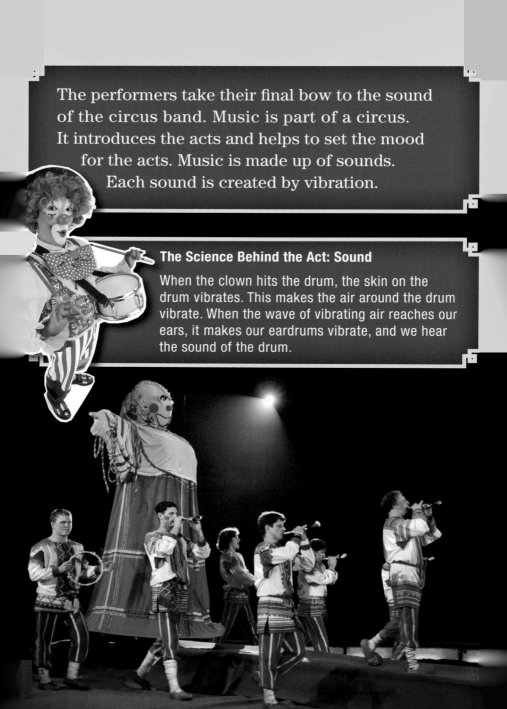

The performers take their final bow to the sound of the circus band. Music is part of a circus. It introduces the acts and helps to set the mood for the acts. Music is made up of sounds. Each sound is created by vibration.

The Science Behind the Act: Sound

When the clown hits the drum, the skin on the drum vibrates. This makes the air around the drum vibrate. When the wave of vibrating air reaches our ears, it makes our eardrums vibrate, and we hear the sound of the drum.

ssary

Index

Informational Explanations

Explanations explain how things work and why things happen.

How to Write an Informational Explanation

Step One

Select a topic.
Make a list of things you know about the topic.
Brainstorm the questions you need to ask.

Circus Science

How do trapeze artists work?

How do jugglers work?

How do tight-rope artists work?

How do acrobats work?

How do the lighting and sound effects work?

Step Two

Research the thing you need to know.

Use different resources for your research.

Internet, Library, Television Documentaries, Experts

Take notes or make copies of what you find.

Step Three

Sort through your notes. Organize related information under specific headings.

Jugglers use the science of gravity

• Gravity pulls objects toward Earth

Juggling

They use the science of force

• Throwing (pushing) things to make them move

They use centripetal force

• Spinning objects at speed to resist the pull of gravity

Step Four

Use your notes to write your Explanation.

• Introduce your topic.
• Add facts, details, and definitions from your research.
• Use quotations, examples, and vocabulary related to the topic.
• Use linking words and phrases, such as *another*, *for example*, *also*, and *because*.
• Provide a conclusion.

a Contents page

an Index

a Glossary

Guide Notes

> **Title: Circus Science**
> **Stage:** Advanced Fluency
> **Text Form:** Informational Explanation
> **Approach**: Guided Reading
> **Processes:** Supporting Comprehension, Exploring Language,
> Processing Information
> **Writing Focus:** Informational Explanation

SUPPORTING COMPREHENSION

- What do you think is the purpose of this book?
- How does the introduction text on page 2 explain the idea behind the topic?
  What do you think the author means by the phrase 'a circus is science at work'?
- How does the diagram on page 6 help the reader understand the science of juggling?
- Do you think it is important for the juggler to be able to assess and practice how hard
  to throw the objects? Why or why not?
- How did the author's example of riding a bike help explain the effect of gravity?
  What other example could be used here?
- How do you think the long pole helps a tight-rope artist keep balanced?
- How does the knowledge of the color spectrum and how to mix primary colors help the
  lighting experts? What effects do certain colors have on people in terms of their mood?
- What connections can you make to mood in music?
- What questions do you have after reading the text?
- Do you think the author effectively conveyed the scientific information in this book?
  Why or why not? What helped you understand the information?

EXPLORING LANGUAGE

Vocabulary
Clarify: daredevils, trapeze, resists, reason, center of gravity, stunning, wavelength
Adverbs: fast, upright
Synonyms: Discuss synonyms for *performers*, *platform*, *reason*, *direction*
Figures of speech: *science at work*

Print conventions
Focus on punctuation: commas to make sense of complex sentences